Proofreading

To find Remedia products in a store near you, go to: **www.rempub.com/stores**

REMEDIA PUBLICATIONS   **SCOTTSDALE, ARIZONA**

Introduction

Proofreading gives students a lot of practice in each of the areas of proofreading.

Symbols are introduced in sequence, starting with the most familiar skill of using capital letters. Rules are presented with examples and followed by extensive practice activities. As each new symbol is presented, it is practiced in isolation and then combined with prior skills. Students are able to build their abilities gradually and in a logical manner.

Upon completion of the exercises in *Proofreading*, students should be able to:

- understand that proofreading is a basic skill applied to all written material.

- use the most common proofreading marks correctly.

- identify instances in writing where mistakes occur.

- rewrite material making corrections where proofreading marks indicate.

- accept that a final copy results after the proofreading and rewrite process is complete.

In the back of this book is a reference booklet to reproduce for each student. It contains the proofreading symbols used in these activities and the most common rules for capitalization and punctuation. If two-sided copies are run, each student can fold one in the center and keep it as a reference source when writing.

In the interest of space, an answer key has not been included in this book. On each page, however, is a number which indicates mistakes to be found on that particular page. Please be aware that, in a few cases, the number could vary because of differences of opinion regarding the use of a comma with introductory elements, the use of a capital letter with a title not followed by a proper name, and the placement of new paragraphs.

The teacher is encouraged to make his or her own answer key and also add or revise punctuation rules if deemed necessary.

Name _____

What is proofreading?

Proofreading is the practice of carefully going over a written report, story, article, or letter before the final copy is made.

You proofread to be sure there are no mistakes. If you find a mistake, you correct it as you proofread.

There are special marks to use as you proofread. The marks are an easy way to show mistakes and how to correct them. You will learn these special marks as you do practice pages.

The mistakes looked for in proofreading are:

- **Capital Letters** — Are capital letters used for the right words?

- **Punctuation** — Are periods, commas, and question marks used in the right places?

- **Sentences** — Are the sentences complete? Do they make good sense? Were any words left out?

- **Spelling** — Are all words spelled correctly?

Answer these questions.

1. When do you proofread? _____

   _____

2. Why do you proofread? _____

   _____

3. If you find a mistake, what do you do? _____

   _____

4. What do you use to make proofreading easier? _____

   _____

5. Name the four things you look for when you proofread.

   _____

   _____

   _____

   _____

Capital Letters

	capitalize

When to use them:

- **at the beginning of every sentence**
- **to begin the name of a special person, place, or thing**
- **to begin names of days, months, and holidays**
- **to begin titles of people (Mr., Dr., Captain)**
- **to begin names of clubs or companies**
- **to begin the first word and all important words in the titles of books, movies, TV shows**
- **for the pronoun I**

Let's practice . . .

Read each sentence below. If a capital letter should be used, make **three short lines** under it. A sample has been done for you.

on monday, we are going to the boys' club.

1. my friend, tony, lives on a farm in ohio.

2. uncle bob is going fishing on the white river.

3. we named our pet mouse rosie.

4. dr. stevens spoke at the pta meeting.

5. next year i will go to ace junior high school.

6. my dad went to work for american airlines last june.

7. have you read the book, *the wizard of oz*?

8. her two best friends are polly and nicole.

9. last christmas we went to salt lake city to ski.

10. i wrote a report about the golden gate bridge.

You should have found 40 words that needed capital letters.

2

Name _____

Proofreading for Capital Letters

If a small letter has been used where a capital is needed, you make **3 short lines** under the small letter.

Examples:

los angeles   miss able   friday

Proofread the sentences below. Use the proofreading mark (☰) where a capital letter should be used. Then, rewrite each sentence on the lines showing the correct capital letters.

1. the gorilla at the ferndale zoo is named boppo.

_____

_____

2. my birthday is on march 14.

_____

3. her favorite TV show is the muppets.

_____

4. when christmas comes, it will snow on oak hill.

_____

5. mrs. mofford is our girl scout leader.

_____

_____

6. last tuesday, aunt sue got a new toyota truck.

_____

_____

You should have found 22 words that needed capital letters.

Name _____

Proofreading for Capital Letters

If a small letter has been used where a capital is needed, you make **3 short lines** under the small letter.

Examples:

christmas   dr. jones   july

Proofread the sentences below. Use the proofreading mark (☰) where a capital letter should be used. Then, re-write each sentence on the lines showing the correct capital letters.

1.   jerry has a new puppy named flip.

_____

2.   we will meet tom at hamburger hut after the game.

_____

_____

3.   many people have tried to climb mount everest.

_____

4.   june 21 is mrs. gilly's birthday.

_____

5.   who is the mayor of chicago, illinois?

_____

6.   we can use lisa's bike to ride to lynx lake.

_____

7.   jeff and brandon will be in dallas on saturday.

_____

8.   i think dr. owen's office is on spruce lane.

_____

You should have found 28 words that needed capital letters.

Proofreading for Capital Letters

If a small letter has been used where a capital is needed, you make **3 short lines** under the small letter.

Examples:

phoenix   mrs. stone   saturday

Proofread the paragraphs below. Use the proofreading mark (≡) where a capital letter should be used.

1. the largest college building on earth is in russia. it is just outside the city of moscow. the building is part of moscow state university. it is 37 stories high.

2. in the year 1843, the first ferris wheel was built in chicago, illinois. the man who built it was named george ferris.

3. there really was a smokey the bear. he was found in new mexico in 1950. he had been badly burned. he lived at the national zoo in washington, d.c., for 26 years.

4. mt. rushmore is in the black hills of south dakota. the heads of four presidents have been carved in the rock. the presidents are washington, jefferson, lincoln, and teddy roosevelt.

5. march 15 is a very special day in hinckley, ohio. it is buzzard day. on this day the buzzards return to hinckley.

6. death valley is the hottest place in north or south america. it is in california. at one time the temperature was 134 degrees.

You should have found a total of 57 words that needed capital letters.

Name _____

Proofreading for Capital Letters

Proofread each short paragraph below. Use the proofreading mark (⊟) under small letters that should be capitals.

1. susan and her family are going to england this summer. they will also go to scotland if they have time. they will be gone all of july and august.

2. next sunday we are giving a surprise party for my uncle jim. cindy and i planned it. we told him to meet us at cave park at two o'clock to play ball. he is going to be surprised to see the whole jackson family there!

3. two weeks ago, we got a new puppy. we named him freckles. mr. hacker gave him to us. he said to feed freckles alpo puppy chow until he is six months old.

4. i have a summer job. i am delivering papers for the hampton news. i work every day except sunday. my dad says to save my money for college.

5. mr. barber owns barber's bike shop. on the fourth of july, he is going to be on the mack sims sports show on TV. he will draw a name to see who wins a new bike. i hope it's me!

6. our class at washington middle school went on a trip to disneyland. the best ride was the matterhorn. we had a great time. i had my picture taken with mickey mouse.

7. last saturday, billy and jason went to see the movie, *who framed roger rabbit*. while they were there, they each had a pepsi and a package of chuckles. billy's dad picked them up after the movie in his new ford bronco.

You should have found 74 words that needed capital letters.

Name _____

Proofreading for Capital Letters

Read the paragraph below. No capital letters have been used. Use the proofreading mark (≡) to show which letters should be capitals. Then write the paragraph correctly on the lines. **There are 24 words that need capital letters.**

the disappearing island

falcon island is really the peak of a volcano. it is about 2,000 miles east of australia. it is in the pacific ocean. in 1913, the volcano erupted. it made the ocean floor shift. this pulled falcon island under the water in 1926. the volcano erupted under water and falcon island reappeared. twenty-three years later, another eruption made falcon island disappear under the pacific island again! no one knows when it may come back.

_____

_____

_____

_____

_____

_____

_____

Name _____

Proofreading for Capital Letters

Sometimes capital letters are used where they are not supposed to be.

In proofreading, (/) means "make this a lower case letter."

Example:

My Ⱦeacher is Miss Brown.

Read the sentences below. If a capital is used where it shouldn't be, use the proofreading mark (/).

1. Jack's house is the gray One on Elm Street.

2. Mom let us get a Pizza for our Party.

3. Ellen's baby Rabbit is named Nibbles.

4. Robbie and I were wading in the Creek.

5. The zoo keeper fed hay to the Elephants.

6. Meet me at the Corner of Main Street and Elm Drive.

7. Mark entered a Kite Flying contest at school.

8. Halloween comes in the Month of October.

9. Next Year I will be Ten years old.

10. Deer like to graze in that Meadow.

11. Jim took his Dog for a walk in the Woods.

12. Next Monday is a Holiday.

You should have found 16 words that should not have capital letters.

Name _____

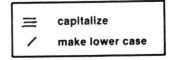
Proofreading for Capital Letters

Use the proofreading marks (≡) (/) to correct the sentences below. Then write the corrected sentences on the lines.

1. Mr. decker drives a big, red Truck to deliver Packages.

    _____

    _____

2. We saw Him come down cooper street and stop at the green House.

    _____

    _____

3. We were not in School because it was saturday.

    _____

    _____

4. We saw a Woodpecker in the tree by bill's house.

    _____

    _____

5. In september, the Grovers are taking a Train ride.

    _____

    _____

6. The play will begin at Seven O'clock on tuesday.

    _____

    _____

7. Do you know the State Bird of texas?

    _____

There are 8 words that need capital letters. There are 11 words that need lower case letters.

Name _____

Proofreading for Capital Letters

Read the paragraph below. Use proofreading marks to correct the use of capital letters. Write the corrected paragraph on the lines.

aztecs

The aztecs were an indian People who lived long Ago in mexico. When Men from spain explored Mexico, they were surprised at how the aztecs lived. they had built a beautiful City. They had an Alphabet and a number System. these indians had Laws and a Strong government. We still enjoy aztec Art today.

_____

_____

_____

_____

_____

_____

There are 10 words that should have capital letters. There are 9 words that should be lower case letters.

Periods

When to use them:

≡	capitalize
/	make lower case
⊙	make a period
∧	add something

- **at the end of a statement or command**
- **after an abbreviation**

Question Marks

When to use them:

- **at the end of a sentence that asks something**

Let's Practice . . .

Read each sentence below. If a period is needed, use this mark ⊙ to show where it should be.

Example: *My dog has a long tail⊙*   *Dr⊙*

If a question mark is needed, mark it this way *∧̇*   Example: *Why is it so long∧̇*

1. Election Day is always on Tuesday

2. This salad is very good

3. Mr Edwards lives in that house

4. Isn't that a beautiful sunset

5. She is ready to eat lunch

6. How many fish did Dr Finch catch

7. Did any big ones get away

8. The rabbit's name is Floppy

9. How many stars are in the flag

10. Come here and sit down

You should have used 8 ⊙ and 4 ∧̇ .

Name _____

In the sentences below, proofreading marks have been used where there are mistakes.

Write the sentences correctly.

≡	**capitalize**
/	**make lower case**
⊙	**make a period**
∧	**add something**

1. mr⊙ grant bought some /umber⊙
   _____

2. what is that strange-looking bug ∧(?)
   _____

3. I think mrs⊙ hoke's plant needs /ater⊙
   _____

4. he hired joe to /ow the lawn⊙
   _____

5. what is your /avorite color ∧(?)
   _____

6. How did that /irl break her arm ∧(?)
   _____

7. put the top back on the /ox⊙
   _____

8. we heard the /and playing in oak park⊙
   _____

Name _____

Can you proofread the sentences below and find all the mistakes?

Use the correct proofreading marks to show where the mistakes are and what to do about them. Then write each corrected sentence. **There are 28 mistakes.**

≡	capitalize
/	make lower case
⊙	make a period
∧	add something

1. that Sign glows in the dark

   _____

2. may i have a Straw for my milk

   _____

3. Did jim say you could use that

   _____

4. ben helped his Mom mop the floor

   _____

5. this Cake was made by Mrs   springer

   _____

6. Did you find a Home for the kitten

   _____

7. a Dime is worth ten cents

   _____

8. mr   james went to florida in july

   _____

Name _____

Proofread the sentences below. Use the correct marks to show where the mistakes are. Then write the sentences correctly. **There are 31 mistakes.**

≡	capitalize
/	make lower case
⊙	make a period
⋀	add something

1. gary stayed up late on tuesday

    _____

2. He was watching the movie called *fast freddy*

    _____

3. did you see that movie

    _____

4. dad used uncle pete's truck yesterday

    _____

5. we are going on a boy scout Camp-out

    _____

6. mr   and mrs   bonner will go with us

    _____

7. do you know which Lake we are going to see

    _____

8. We will All meet at the cliff street school

    _____

                    ©Remedia Publications

Name _____

Read the short story below. Use the proofreading marks you have learned to show where the mistakes are. Write the story correctly.

There are 21 mistakes.

≡	capitalize
/	make lower case
⊙	make a period
∧	add something

Jessica heard a sound   it came from the edge of the Path. what could it

be   She walked toward the sound and saw a tiny kitten   it was patches

patches belonged to mr wheeler. its back feet were caught in some String   she

helped the kitten and carried it back to mr wheeler's house

_____

_____

_____

_____

_____

_____

_____

Name _____

Commas

≡	capitalize
/	make lower case
⊙	make a period
∧	add something
⋏	add a comma

The comma has more uses than any other punctuation mark.
Below are some of the ways the comma is used.

1) Read each rule. 2) Look at the example. 3) Proofread the
practice sentences. Use ⋏ to show where the commas should
be placed.

Use commas:

- **to separate words or phrases in a series** .
  He has a turtle, a fish, and a bird for pets.

  Practice:

1. I want fudge whipped cream and nuts on my ice cream.

- **to separate *yes, no, well,* or *oh* at the beginning of a sentence** .
  No, I can't go with you.

  Practice:

2. Well maybe I can go for a while.

- **to set off the name of a person spoken to** .
  I'm afraid, John, that you will be late.

  Practice:

3. Your picture is well done Terry.

- **to separate the day of the month from the year in a date** .
  July 20, 1981

  Practice:

4. He was born on October 10 1967.

- **to follow the year when other words follow in the sentence** .
  I left on May 10, 1982, right after the big flood.

  Practice:

5. July 4 1776 is an important date in history.

Proofreading for Commas
and Capital Letters

Read each sentence below. Use the proofreading
marks to show where capital letters and commas
should be. **There are 33 mistakes.**

≡	capitalize
/	make lower case
⊙	make a period
⋏	add something
⋏	add a comma

1. Oh i didn't hear you coming.

2. On March 18 1965 the first russian walked in space.

3. Karen may i have your french fries?

4. The spring months are march april and may.

5. You made the team Martha.

6. My brother was born august 5 1981.

7. Yes I go to mason middle school.

8. We need paper string and wood to make a kite.

9. Well i guess we can go now.

10. denver dallas and atlanta are my favorite teams.

11. No that is not the one I want.

12. please charley stop making that noise.

Name _____

Commas

Below are more ways to use commas.

1) Read each rule. 2) Look at the example.
3) Proofread the practice sentences. Use ∧ to show where the commas should be.

≡	capitalize
/	make lower case
⊙	make a period
∧	add something
⋏	add a comma

Commas are used:

- **to separate an appositive from the rest of the sentence** (an appositive gives more information about a noun).
    Fred, my cousin from Omaha, is coming to visit.

Practice:

1. This is Miss Rawlings my music teacher.

2. Slam Dunk a game we made up is really fun.

- **to separate a city, state, or country** .
    We went to Seattle, Washington, to see the Space Needle.

Practice:

3. Paris France is a beautiful city.

4. My uncle's ranch is in Cheyenne Wyoming.

- **when you use *and, but,* or *or* to join two sentences** .
    I ran to the bus stop, but I was too late.

Practice:

5. Hold on tightly or you will fall.

6. We sang the song and Mickey danced.

Name _____

Proofreading for Commas
and Capital Letters

Read each sentence. Use the proofreading marks
to show where the commas and capital letters
belong. **There are 31 mistakes.**

≡	capitalize
/	make lower case
⊙	make a period
∧	add something
⩘	add a comma

1. There are many beaches near Charleston south carolina.

2. Wizard my brother's pet lizard got out of his cage.

3. I saw a flying saucer and it was really big.

4. Bruce worked on his project and he won first place.

5. The Circus world Museum is in Baraboo wisconsin.

6. It rained hard but we enjoyed our picnic anyway.

7. james madison our fourth President was born March 16 1751.

8. The cheetah jaguar and gorilla are endangered animals.

9. my aunt alice lives in nashville tennessee.

10. You may go Fred after you mow the lawn.

11. I'm going to baseball camp or I'm going to the beach.

12. my best friend arthur can wiggle his ears.

Name _____

The sentences below have been proofread. Look carefully at the marks and write the sentences correctly on the lines.

≡	capitalize
/	make lower case
⊙	make a period
∧	add something
⌄	add a comma

1. mike please go with david and the boys.

   _____

2. he raises geese Ducks and chickens.

   _____

3. On saturday june 15 we leave for Camp.

   _____

4. can you be ready in five Minutes Sally?

   _____

5. The game is over and steve is leaving.

   _____

6. we visited uncle Sid in reno nevada.

   _____

7. Dr. Billings will see you now jennifer.

   _____

8. she went to mack's bike shop on elm street.

   _____

Name _____

The sentences below will help you practice using all the proofreading marks you have learned so far.

Use the correct mark to show where a mistake has been made. Write each sentence correctly on the line. **There are 28 mistakes.**

=	capitalize
/	make lower case
⊙	make a period
∧	add something
⋏	add a comma

1. Rick ben becky and sarah are on the Bus

   _____

2. Al are you eating lunch now

   _____

3. On Monday december 5 the Twins will be 10 years old

   _____

4. Well i guess you can have One more

   _____

5. You can come in but you should wipe your feet

   _____

6. Our team Captain Janis made the winning run

   _____

7. Where is my surfer magazine brad

   _____

Name _____

Use the proofreading marks to correct the paragraphs below. Then write the paragraphs correctly on the lines.

≡	capitalize
/	make lower case
⊙	make a period
∧	add something
⋏	add a comma

There are 15 mistakes in paragraph one.

There are 10 mistakes in paragraph two.

The newspaper said a giant Sea Serpent had been found on the beach near boston massachusetts many people went to see the strange Beast. a scientist examined it carefully It was a rare Shark one not usually found near the united states

_____

_____

_____

_____

_____

_____

Many famous composers came from germany a country in Europe the music of mozart wagner and bach is played all over the world

_____

_____

_____

_____

Name _____

Use the proofreading marks you have learned to correct the paragraphs below. Then write the paragraphs correctly on the lines.

≡	capitalize
/	make lower case
⊙	make a period
∧	add something
⋏	add a comma

Paragraph one has 7 mistakes.

Paragraph two has 13 mistakes.

Alaska was a very good buy It cost the united states about two cents an acre. in may, 1867, we bought alaska from russia for seven million dollars.

_____

_____

_____

_____

Warren harding the 29th President of the united states really liked dogs He had a dog named laddie boy Harding gave his dog a birthday party at the white house. the birthday cake was made of dog biscuits and they were covered with frosting.

_____

_____

_____

_____

_____

Name _____

The short report below has many mistakes. Look carefully at the proofreading marks and write the paragraph correctly.

In the western united states, there are some strange Plants. One is a spiny, round, bushy weed. it is the tumbleweed. Tumbleweeds grow on the north american deserts. In the fall, when the plant gets very dry, the stem breaks off at the Ground. the Wind blows the plant for many miles. would you be surprised to see a plant rolling down the Highway?

_____

_____

_____

_____

_____

_____

_____

Name _____

The short report below has many mistakes. Use the proofreading marks you have learned to show how to correct it. Then write the report correctly on the lines. **There are 18 mistakes.**

kangaroos

Kangaroos can be found all over australia A baby kangaroo is called a joey the first thing a newborn joey does is find its way into its Mother's pouch it climbs into the pouch and it stays there for many Months. it will be warm and safe a joey sleeps drinks its mother's milk and bounces along wherever She goes. doesn't that sound like a nice life

_____

_____

_____

_____

_____

_____

_____

_____

Name _____

Use proofreading marks to correct the report below. Then write the report correctly on the lines. **There are 14 mistakes.**

volcanoes

a Volcano is a cone-shaped mountain with an opening at the top a volcano erupts and there is a loud explosion. then ashes steam gases and hot, melted rock are forced out the opening. The hot, melted rock that pours from the Volcano is called Fire lava. Then it cools and it hardens to stone

_____

_____

_____

_____

_____

_____

_____

Incomplete Sentences

When you proofread, it is important to be sure all sentences are complete and correct. Sometimes sentences are not complete. They don't tell a whole thought or idea.

An incomplete sentence . . .

- **does not tell a complete thought.**

    My new bike.

- **has words left out.**

    She stepped the mud.

Read each sentence below. If it does not tell a complete thought, draw a line through it and use the **take out** mark. **There are 7 incomplete sentences.**

Example: ~~My new bike.~~

1. We rode the waves.

2. Found it yesterday.

3. Mary won the race.

4. My oldest brother.

5. The house on the corner.

6. It crawled slowly.

7. All the way to school.

8. Old are you?

9. Kept it very warm.

10. I want that.

11. Beside the elephant.

12. Who told you?

Top-right proofreading marks box:

≡	capitalize
/	make lower case
⊙	make a period
∧	add something
⩗	add a comma
℮	take out

Proofread the sentences below. If a word has been left out, use this mark ∧ and add a word to make each sentence complete.

Example: She stepped⟨over⟩the mud.

≡	capitalize
/	make lower case
⊙	make a period
∧	add something
⋏	add a comma
⌐	take out

1. Martha off the stage.

2. Dad gave a new bike.

3. He needs more green for the fence.

4. Will go with us?

5. Mom made Bill put on coat.

6. The squirrel's was high in the tree.

7. A careless camper caused forest fire.

8. New babies a lot.

9. I will my homework later.

10. Dark hung in the sky.

11. Joe had a on his knee.

12. The sun rises in the east and in the west.

Proofreading for Incomplete Sentences

Use proofreading marks and complete the sentences below. Then write the sentence correctly on the line.

≡	capitalize
/	make lower case
⊙	make a period
∧	add something
⋏	add a comma
℮	take out

Example:

The boy with the sled.

Step 1: take out the period ℮

Step 2: add words to make the sentence complete ∧

Step 3: put the period back in at the end of the sentence ⊙

is my friend⊙
The boy with the sled ℮∧

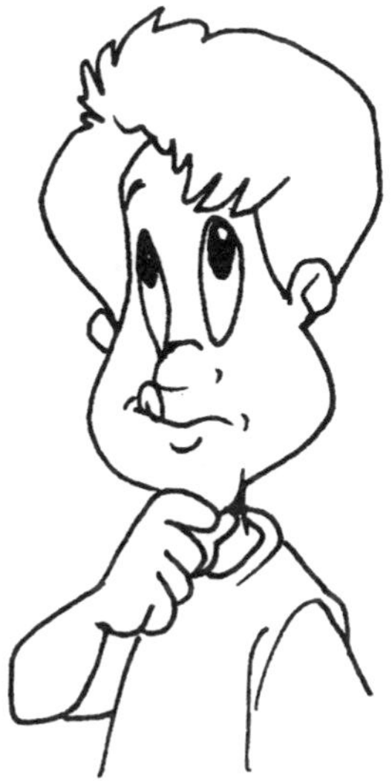

1. My two sisters are.

_____

2. The hamster got.

_____

3. I think you.

_____

4. The party dress.

_____

5. All five of them.

_____

6. Our trip to Disneyland.

_____

Proofreading for Incomplete Sentences

Use proofreading marks and added words to complete each sentence below. Then write the sentence correctly on the line.

☰	capitalize
/	make lower case
⊙	make a period
∧	add something
⋏	add a comma
ℰ	take out

Example:

The boy with the sled.

Step 1: Change the capital at the beginning of the sentence to a lower case letter.

Step 2: Add words to make the sentence complete. Be sure to capitalize the first word of the sentence.

We saw
∧*The boy with the sled.*

1. Made a doghouse.

_____

2. Celebrate his birthday.

_____

3. Can open the door.

_____

4. Won the relay race.

_____

5. Kept in a big cage.

_____

6. Told me a secret.

_____

Proofreading for Run-On Sentences

	capitalize
/	make lower case
⊙	make a period
𝗄	add something
𝖼	add a comma
~	take out

As you proofread, watch for run-on sentences. Run-on sentences are two sentences put together as one.

Example:

Her dog is brown he has white spots.

Should be:

Her dog is brown. He has white spots.

Read the run-on sentences below. Use proof-reading marks to show where the mistakes are. Write the sentences correctly on the lines. **There are 25 mistakes.**

1. Your story is spooky I am scared.

   _____

2. Will you come with us we are going to the Park.

   _____

3. My Birthday is next week i can't wait

   _____

4. Ed's sick he won't be in school today.

   _____

5. our team had Batting practice mr kerns pitched

   _____

6. these toys are broken shall I throw them away

   _____

7. can we feed the Elephant peanuts he likes them.

   _____

Name _____

Watch for run-on sentences in the short paragraph below. Use the proofreading marks you have learned to show the mistakes. Then write the paragraph correctly on the lines.
There are 9 mistakes.

Safe drinking water is something. we all need America has many lakes and rivers for drinking water. But over the years, our water supply has been growing. Less and less safe. We need to clean up our lakes and rivers we need to care about our water. if we don't, we will have no more? Beautiful, clean water.

_____

_____

_____

_____

_____

_____

_____

_____

_____

Name _____

Use the proofreading marks you have learned to show where the mistakes are in the paragraph below. Then write the paragraph correctly on the lines. **There are 22 mistakes.**

color

Years ago people thought things looked. colorful because they had color in them. about 1700 a man from england sir isaac newton made a Discovery. he proved the that things look colorful because of the way light? Bounces off them. he held a prism a triangle of glass up to a window. The prism bent the light into see seven parts. each part was a different color?

_____

_____

_____

_____

_____

_____

_____

_____

Name _____

Use proofreading marks to show where the mistakes are. Then write the paragraph correctly on the lines. **There are 18 mistakes.**

bacteria

bacteria are very tiny living things. they can live almost anywhere they live in cold Oceans hot places and even the Air around us. they like to where they can find food some live in fresh milk fish or meat Others like Garbage or dead leaves. Some even live in your body

_____

_____

_____

_____

_____

_____

_____

_____

Proofreading for Misspelled Words

Another reason to proofread is to correct any words that are not spelled correctly.

The mark used is ——— with the word spelled correctly above it.

Example:

Don't spell ~~words rong.~~ *words wrong*

Look for the misspelled words in the sentences below. Use proofreading marks and correct them. **There are 24 misspelled words.**

1. When did you loose you're puppy?

2. He hert his leg wen he fell.

3. That gril had really long hare.

4. Do you know who evented the radioh?

5. There was a jiant storm last nite.

6. Sam racked the leafs into a pile.

7. We had tree minutes to git the bus.

8. She din't fell well after the boat ride.

9. Bring the dishes two the sink, plese.

10. A map is hepful when takeing a trip.

11. The bird taped the tree with its beek.

12. We safed our monney for new skates.

≡	capitalize
/	make lower case
⊙	make a period
∧	add something
⋀	add a comma
⌐	take out
—	make a change

Name _____

Proofreading for Capital Letters and Misspelled Words

Read the sentences below. Use proofreading marks to correct spelling mistakes and capital letters. **There are 41 mistakes.**

=	**capitalize**
/	**make lower case**
⊙	**make a period**
⋏	**add something**
⋏	**add a comma**
℈	**take out**
—	**make a change**

1. sarah is backing a cake four tim's Party.

2. The Clock stricks every our.

3. the Fan blue ann's hat of.

4. We are going to lake erie in Ogust.

5. the smith family want to england.

6. I realy lick the story, stone soup.

7. this is roger's dog, Scamp.

8. Melissa skooped the ice scream from the Bowl.

9. Tom, Sam, and ed sleppt in our bake yard.

10. i start swiming lessons next Satday.

11. When the bell rang, madison school was verry quite.

12. You were very nise to fix me a samwich.

Name _____

Use all your proofreading marks in the paragraphs below. Then write the paragraphs correctly on the lines. **Paragraph one has 12 mistakes. Paragraph two has 11 mistakes.**

Jack and his Brother wated for a bus Many cars and Trucks went by but the bus din't com. jack was getting angrey At last the bus came into sigt. Both boys felled better.

_____

_____

_____

_____

the koto a musical instrument came form japan. it is shaped like a long, flat box It has many strengs stretched along the top. the koto is laid on the player's lap and he plucks the strengs.

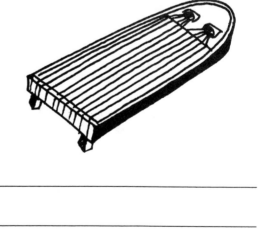

_____

_____

_____

_____

Name _____

Proofread the paragraphs below. Use proofreading marks to show where the corrections should be. Then write the paragraphs correctly on the lines. **Paragraph one has 15 mistakes. Paragraph two has 17 mistakes.**

≡	capitalize
/	make lower case
⊙	make a period
⋏	add something
⋏	add a comma
⊸	take out
—	make a change

Big storms can cause a of trouble It is important that people are warned early about hurricanes. several plains called Hurricane Hunters are always in the air during hurricane season in the united states, this season lasts from june to november. the Planes have special equipment two gather information about Big Storms.

_____

_____

_____

_____

Rachel carson was born in springdale pennsylvania. She rote books about life in and around the oceans. Won of her books the silent spring warned about using insecticides it talls of the harm they to Man and Animals.

_____

_____

_____

_____

Name _____

The report below has been proofread for you.
Read it carefully. Then write the report correctly
on the lines. Make all the corrections marked.

≡	capitalize
/	make lower case
⊙	make a period
∧	add something
∧	add a comma
ℯ	take out
—	make a change

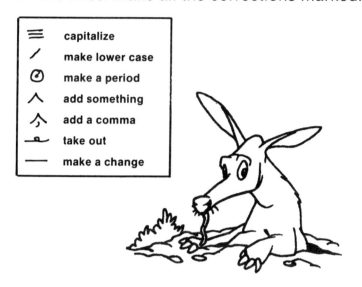

the Ardvark

The aardvark is a strange creature its name comes form the dutch word that meaning earth-pig it is the size of a hog and it has thick, grayish hair. It has long ears like a rabbit.

the aardvark digs a hole and he sleeps during the day at night he hunts for food he ets tiny ants and termites. He ters open the nests with his sharp clause and gobbles up insects with his long, stiky tongue

_____

_____

_____

_____

_____

_____

_____

_____

_____

Proofreading for Paragraphs

The report below looks like one paragraph. It should be two paragraphs.

Read the report carefully. Decide where a new paragraph should begin. Use the proofreading mark (ᕼ) in front of the word that should begin the new paragraph. Use the other proofreading marks you have learned to show where corrections should be made.

There are 12 mistakes.

☰	capitalize
/	make lower case
⊙	make a period
∧	add something
⋏	add a comma
⸺	take out
—	make a change
ᕼ	begin a paragraph

There is a strange turtle that lives the Ocean It is the alligator snapping turtle. This animal has a long, pink streak in the middle of its tongue It looks just like a worm. fish swim right into its mouth to get the worm. Alligator turtles live in the southern united states. they can weigh up to 150 pounds they eat only fish. They can stay buried in the sand with no food for weeks at a time

40

Name _____

Read the report below. Use your proofreading marks to show all the mistakes. There should be two paragraphs. Use the ¶ sign to show where the second paragraph begins. Then write the report correctly on the lines.

There are 15 mistakes.

Bees live together in a colony. In a bee colony, there is won queen many drones and thousands of workers All workers are female bees. thay do all the work for the colony They take care of Young Bees. they gather swet juices from flours. They even make the honeycomb the place where the Queen's eggs are laid.

_____

_____

_____

_____

_____

_____

_____

Name _____

There are two paragraphs in this report. There are also some mistakes with capital letters, punctuation, and spelling. Find the mistakes and use proofreading marks to show where they are. Then write the report correctly on the lines.

There are 22 mistakes.

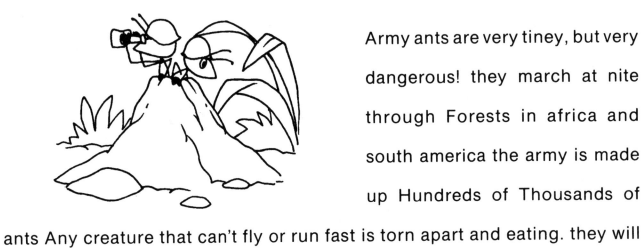

Army ants are very tiney, but very dangerous! they march at nite through Forests in africa and south america the army is made up Hundreds of Thousands of ants Any creature that can't fly or run fast is torn apart and eating. they will attak scorpions tarantulas and wounded or sick animals of eny size! this army means business!

_____

_____

_____

_____

_____

_____

_____

_____

Name _____

This report will help you practice proofreading. It is one paragraph. Find all the mistakes and use your proofreading marks to show where they are. Then write the report correctly on the lines and give it a title.

There are 20 mistakes.

Sneezing makes you push a qick Puff of air threw you're mouth and noze. you might get a sneezing spell from a clod a bit of dust or a tickel inside your noze We are never sure what causes a snese or when we will sneeze. we allso don't no what Noise will come out even if we trie to stop the sound

_____

_____

_____

_____

_____

_____

_____

_____

Name _____

Read the report below. It has two paragraphs. There are also other mistakes for you to find and mark. After you have proofread the report, write it correctly on the lines.

There are 25 mistakes.

Windmills can be fond all over the world they are very tall and they have weels on top. the wind terns the weels and the mills pump water somethings they make Electricity. Holland has meny windmills and so does the united states ef you take a drive in the contry, you may some windmills on farms that you pass

_____

_____

_____

_____

_____

_____

_____

_____

_____

Proofreading Letters

It is important to proofread letters. Mistakes make them very hard to read! The letter below has been proofread. Write the letter correctly on the lines.

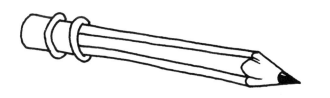

4702 <u>s</u>lider <u>s</u>treet

<u>d</u>allas, <u>t</u>exas

<u>o</u>ctober 20, 1988

dear mr clink,

          writing
i am ~~writeing~~ to ask you to send me a copy of your book, the happy camper.

My friend has one, and I think it looks like a good book. it has lots of interesting

   in ¶   money
ideas it. I saved the ~~muney~~ from my allowance until I had seven ̷dollars.

              truly
yours turly,

Cindy Scout

☰	capitalize
/	make lower case
⊙	make a period
∧	add something
⋏	add a comma
ℯ	take out
—	make a change
¶	begin a paragraph

_____

_____

_____

_____

_____

_____

_____

_____

Name _____

Proofread the letter below. Then write it correctly on the lines.
There are 23 mistakes.

☰	capitalize
/	make lower case
⊙	make a period
人	add something
人	add a comma
⊶	take out
—	make a change

724 e state street

denver colorado

May 10 1988

dear uncle bill,

    Thank you for the monopoly game you sent me for my Birthday. it is really

fun play. My friends all went to come over to try it out I had great Party. we went

boling I got 142 for my score

                    your nephew,

                    Chuck

_____

_____

_____

_____

_____

_____

_____

_____

Name _____

Proofread the letter below. Write it correctly on the lines. **There are 33 mistakes.**

618 n. evans avenue

toledo ohio

february 10 1988

dear carrie,

    how do you lick your new school we miss having you in room 12. we are bisy making projects for science fair It will be in march our team one the Baseball Trophy last week. we were all very happy please right and tell us about you're new house and the kids your class

                          your friend,

                          sarah

_____

_____

_____

_____

_____

_____

_____

                          _____

                          _____

Name _____

Proofread the book report below. Use your proofreading marks to show where the corrections should be made.

There are 28 mistakes.

how the camel got his hump

by rudyard kipling

this is a story that happened way back wen the world was was new. the Camel did

not have a hump. yet. he was very lazey and he did not want to Work All the other

aminals were busy helping man. When thay asked him to help, the camel said,

"Humph." The animals talked to asked the Genie of the Desert to help them. he

did he gave the camel a Hump on his back and made him work hard

Name _____

As you proofread, you can also change words to make your writing more interesting. One way to add interest is to use different action words (verbs).

Read the sentences below. The action word (verb) has been underlined. Can you find a more interesting word to use in its place? Use the take-out mark and the word box to help you.

=	capitalize
/	make lower case
⊙	make a period
∧	add something
⋏	add a comma
⸜	take out
—	make a change
¶	begin a paragraph

swooped
shouted
swirled
burst
flew
chattered
crouched
glided
asked
clanged
prowled
crash
dashed
streaked
sneaked
stared
perched
went
wiggled
tinkled

1. We all looked at the strange creature.

2. The hawk flew down after the mouse.

3. The panther sat on the rock and waited.

4. "Stop where you are," said the guard.

5. The leaves blew down the street.

6. Mom heard the cookie jar fall to the floor.

7. Brad was excited as he came into the room.

8. The bored children moved in their chairs.

9. The bell in the tower rang loudly.

10. The jet went across the sky.

11. The excited ladies all talked at once.

12. The fox walked quietly through the woods.

Name _____

Describing words make your writing more interesting. The sentences below have *boring* words in them. Take these words out and replace each one with a better word. You may want to use the words in the box. Proofread the sentences as you go. Then write the sentences correctly on the lines.

scramble	threw	sprang
rolled	grabbed	streaked
scattered	trickled	moved
snatched	flashed	tumbled

There are 14 mistakes.

1. jean put seeds on the ground for the Birds.

    _____

2. harry got to his feet wen he heard the crash

    _____

3. In dry Weather, the creek ran very little.

    _____

4. Lightning crossed through the dark Sky

    _____

5. we saw dan go quickly up the steep rocks

    _____

6. Suddenly, mark's lite went on by itself

    _____

Name _____

Proofread the story below. Use all the proofreading marks.
Write the story correctly on the lines.

There are 48 mistakes.

a scary story

once upon a time, rob bob and louise wanted a pizza they decided to go to the
pizza palace up on hoover hill. The Pizza palace had good pizza. To get there,
they had to go over bumpy bridge. a bad troll lived under Bridge. he was
hungry, two. Wen he herd footsteps on the bridge, he came out and said he was
going eat the Children. rob bob and louise were afraid but then louise had idea.
She asked the trol if he would rather have a Pizza he said he only liked pizza
with marshamllows and Dill Pickles. when the children said they would bring
him won, he let them go they all live happily ever after.

_____

_____

_____

_____

_____

_____

_____

_____

_____

_____

_____

_____

Name _____

Proofread the story below. Use all the proofreading marks.
Write the story correctly on the lines.

There are 26 mistakes.

the country store

in the old days, many towns were sew small they had olny one store These

country stores were very important they were busy places The country store

sold food clothes tools and Animal fed. a person could buy pots pans paint and

fishing poles. people got their mail at the stores and they visited with their

neighbors. country Stores were busy places when america was young

_____

_____

_____

_____

_____

_____

_____

_____

_____

_____

_____

_____

_____

Proofreading Symbols

≡	make a capital letter
/	make a lower case letter
⊙	add a period
∧	add something
∧,	add a comma
ℓ	take out
—	make a change
¶	begin a paragraph

- **separates the day of the month from the year in a date.**

  June 5, 1988

- **follows the year when other words follow in the sentence.**

  Her vacation started May 2, 1988, and ended two weeks later.

- **separates an appositive from the rest of the sentence. (An appositive tells more about a noun.)**

  Casey Jones, a railroad engineer, was born in 1864.

  Spring, when the weather gets nice, is my favorite season.

- **separates a city from a state or country.**

  We live in Phoenix, Arizona.

  The first Olympics were in Athens, Greece.

- **separates two sentences that are connected with *and, but,* or *or.***

  I wanted to go, but it was too late.

CAPITALIZATION

A Capital Letter:

- **begins a sentence.**

  She is a good friend.

- **begins the name of a special person, place, or thing.**

  Disneyland is in Anaheim, California.

- **begins names of days, months, and holidays.**

  Thanksgiving is on the last Thursday in November.

- **begins titles of people.**

  Mr.   Miss   Dr.

- **begins names of clubs or companies.**

  Camp Fire Girls   Radio Shack

- **begins the first word and all important words in the titles of books, movies, TV shows.**

  Rabbit Hill   Superman II   Facts of Life

- **is used for the pronoun I.**

  When the bell rings, I will leave.

PUNCTUATION

A Period:

- **ends a statement or command.**

  This is my seat.

  Hang up your jacket.

- **follows an abbreviation.**

  Mon.   Dec.   Mr.

A Question Mark:

- **ends an asking sentence.**

  What time is it?

A Comma:

- **separates words or phrases in a series.**

  She works on Monday, Tuesday, and Friday.

- **separates *yes, no, well,* or *oh* at the beginning of a sentence.**

  No, he isn't here now.

- **sets off the name of a person spoken to.**

  I heard, Jim, that your team won.